MUSEUMS & GALLERIES
COMMISSION

Showing the Flag

*Loans from National Museums
to the Regions*

David M. Wilson

A report commissioned with
financial assistance from
the Calouste Gulbenkian Foundation
London 1992

LONDON: HMSO

© Crown copyright 1992

Applications for reproduction should be made
to HMSO

First published 1992

ISBN 0 11 290515 3

British Library Cataloguing in Publication Data

A CIP catalogue record for this book is
available from the British Library

*(Front cover) From an original cartoon by Larry,
reproduced by permission of the Punch Library.*

Contents

Contents *continued*

Foreword

by the Chairman of the Museums & Galleries Commission

The report which follows is concerned with loans from the national collections, and how to make these collections available to regional audiences. The Commission has long argued that the national museums should lend more and more readily to museums in the regions. Sir David estimates that something like £1 million is needed to enable the national museums to maintain and expand their loan programmes, including travelling exhibitions. Travelling or – as Sir David likes to call them – loan exhibitions do much more than make the national collections available to regional audiences. Non-national museums rely on changing exhibitions from a wide variety of sources to attract and maintain media and public interest. Touring is one of the most cost-effective ways of sharing knowledge and resources for the benefit of a wider public; it is also one of the most obvious ways in which central government can contribute directly to cultural life outside the capital cities and throughout the United Kingdom.

Sir David's brief was to consider loan exhibitions solely from the national collections. However, we should not lose sight of the wider picture, for the majority of exhibitions mounted in the regions have little or no input from the national museums. In this context, it is worth recalling that a report last year on the MGC, commissioned by the Office of Arts and Libraries, indicated that the MGC needed a minimum of £500,000 to continue properly the work of its Travelling Exhibitions Unit.

At a time when the MGC's own budget for travelling exhibitions was fully spent, the Calouste Gulbenkian Foundation expressed an interest in what we were attempting to do, as part of its concern to encourage access in general. On behalf of the MGC, I should like to thank the Foundation for support which made the research possible, and to thank in particular the Director of the UK Branch, Ben Whitaker, for his help.

We are also grateful to Sir David Wilson for the characteristic enthusiasm with which he responded to our invitation and for the zest with which he has gone round the national museums and produced within a short period a report which, unlike many today, is readable and eminently practical in its recommendations.

GRAHAM GREENE

Preface

In asking me to write this report, the Museums & Galleries Commission gave me a brief:

To examine the options for encouraging wider access to the national collections by means of travelling exhibitions and loans of individual items and complete exhibitions.

I have ranged widely in the field to construct a report which I trust, within the limits of time and space allowed me, reflects accurately the opinions of my professional colleagues and gives some idea of a way forward in bringing material from the national museums to the provinces.

In addition to my formal brief, I was asked to pay particular attention to the possibility of increasing the number of loans containing three-dimensional objects – in other words, cased exhibitions – it being quite rightly felt that in general it is cheaper and therefore easier for the borrower to mount exhibitions of paintings, watercolours, prints, drawings and photographs.

It has been no part of my task to examine other travelling exhibition or loan services. I have not, for example, considered in more than cursory fashion the excellent loans provided by the South Bank Centre (formerly the touring programme of the Arts Council) or by the area museum councils.

Because of the limited period at my disposal, my research has perforce been quick and largely based on personal interviews. Although many museums and institutions (including all the national museums and galleries) have provided me with written evidence, I have not been able to tabulate that material in this report. My appendices may therefore seem eccentric, but they have important relevance to what I have tried to say.

Throughout this report I have followed common practice in using the term 'museum' as a portmanteau term for both museums and art galleries.

DAVID M WILSON

National treasures and the regions

An open letter to the Rt Hon Peter Brooke, Secretary of State for the National Heritage

Dear Secretary of State,

The enormous wealth of the collections held in the nineteen national museums and galleries is only surpassed by the wide variety of interests represented in them. The museums attract millions of visitors each year – visitors who come from all parts of the world and from every corner of the United Kingdom; visitors of all ages and every social class. The services they offer are second to none: their collections are open to everybody; the scholarship upon which they are founded is the envy of the world; and their standards of display, education and outreach are of the highest quality.

A major element of outreach spearheaded by the national museums has been the mounting of special exhibitions of international importance. The public first became impressed by this phenomenon in 1972, when the extraordinary success of the *Tutankhamun* exhibition at the British Museum made front-page news and raised the consciousness of the British public towards museums.

Tutankhamun was but one episode in a series of exhibitions of increasing popularity and sophistication mounted by the national museums, the Arts Council and the Royal Academy which have introduced international art and culture to an extraordinarily wide public. The success of these exhibitions revolutionised the nation's attitude to museums. Once perceived as dusty and drab, museums are now seen as lively, bustling and innovative.

Such exhibitions and their stylish manner of display had a considerable influence on the large number of regional museums in Britain. Although these museums had themselves frequently mounted great exhibitions, the public outside London now demanded bigger and better shows. And the public got them. Perhaps the most extraordinary success was achieved by the Yorkshire Museum in York which in 1982, against all odds, was able to mount an exhibition of international importance on the *Vikings in England* which attracted 320,000 visitors.

National museums lent enthusiastically to this exhibition, as they have done to many other shows over the years, an enthusiasm demonstrated by the fact that during 1991 only about 5% of the thousands of formal requests for loans received from the regions (normally for loans to exhibitions being arranged by regional curators) have been turned down by national museums. Given the resources, there is now a great opportunity to extend the national museums' role in the regions through a developed loan exhibition programme.

Loan exhibitions make the collections of the national museums available for display in the museums of the regions. They share knowledge and resources for the benefit of a wider public. The national museums and their regional counterparts wholeheartedly share this vision. They lack only the financial ability to fulfil it. While individual museums are able to present individual bids, the Museums & Galleries Commission is well placed to formulate proposals on a national scale. It was against this background that the MGC, with the generous support of the Gulbenkian Foundation, asked me to prepare this report.

The type of loans discussed in this report vary from minimal long-term deposits which fill a gap in a regional museum's permanent display to full-blown exhibitions of objects of international importance. The national museums wish to expand their outreach by making available to the regions more prime objects – not merely their secondary collections – and further wish to provide complete exhibitions on a greater scale, together with a back-up of educational packages and publications. Many of the services are already provided on a small scale. But with vision it would be possible to increase public access to the rich treasures of the national collections.

An attractive idea, for example, is the possibility of lending major acquisitions, bought through the National Heritage Memorial Fund and the National Art Collections Fund, to a number of regional centres before they are put on permanent display in the national museum. Would it not be splendid, for example, for tax-payers in the regions to see works of art like Holbein's *A Lady with a Squirrel and a Starling* and the *Armada Service* which have recently been acquired by the nation? This cannot, however, be achieved without fresh resources.

This report examines in detail the parameters and problems of lending material from national to regional museums; it also suggests solutions. If the national museums were allowed to bid against an annual sum of £1 million, they would be able to provide access to national treasures housed in national museums on a scale never previously realized.

I would most warmly commend this proposal to you as it clearly and fully measures up to the ideas you and your predecessors have expressed concerning the need to extend public access to the arts and to the heritage.

Yours sincerely
DAVID M WILSON

1 Conceptions and misconceptions

1.1   It is a long held and honourable tenet of all national museums and galleries in this country that (in the words of the founding trustees of the British Museum in 1753), *the collections be kept for the benefit of the public who may have free access to peruse the same*. Although this statement is interpreted in many ways by the various national museums, it (or something like it) remains central to their beliefs and activities.   One of these activities – more recently developed than most – is the provision of loans to museums at home and abroad.   This outreach is clearly an extension of the objective of access and is of prime importance in a country in which a great deal of taxpayers' money is invested in museums, and where an ever more sophisticated and educated public flocks to special exhibitions. It is time to try and lay down a few general guidelines on individual loans and loan exhibitions and to calculate the cost of increasing their number by making the rich and extensive collections of the national museums more widely available in the regions.   The Museums & Galleries Commission, which is the government's official advisory body on all aspects of museums, is clearly the right body to look at this problem.

1.2   There are many misconceptions concerning the attitude of the national museums to regional museums.   In no area is this more patent than in relation to loans of exhibition material.   It cannot be stressed too emphatically that, while practices differ and circumstances vary, there is no national institution which does not value its contacts with regional colleagues and which is not willing to lend material to them.   Their inhibitions concern the condition of the object in relation to travel and display, together with the state of security in the host institution.   In most cases, national institutions give preference to regional loans as against international loans and are totally committed to such outreach.   Only ever growing limitation of resources and internal priorities in the use of staff and money limit the expansion of loan services. All national museums, including all those who already do so, expressed the wish to be able to lend or to continue to lend whole exhibitions to the regions.   Only the Natural History Museum felt that there was no demand for their services as exhibition-providers (although they lend specimens freuently and have recently had good publicity in the professional

9

press for their Travelling Discovery Centre – more a travelling educational tool than an exhibition proper – which during 1991–92 visited centres in Northern Ireland as well as the Stranraer Museum). In this context the National Museums and Galleries on Merseyside has recently set up a network known as the Botanical Touring Exhibitions Group which mainly consists of national institutions (including the botanical gardens and the Natural History Museum) to encourage botanical exhibitions.

1.3   The commitment of the national museums to loans is considerable and on-going. The Victoria and Albert Museum, for example, has recently calculated that it costs them £250,000 yearly to administer requested loans. National museums and galleries accept that loans to the regions are an important element of their function. All they need to generate this function are resources, which in the present public spending climate are difficult to find.

1.4   In general, national museums feel that they have established good relationships with their regional colleagues. Hardly a day goes by when national and regional museums do not consult each other – freely and with great friendliness on all sides. The average museum curator – national or provincial – is a fanatical museum visitor and, moving around the country, will naturally visit any museum he or she passes and will often talk with the curator on such visits. There is a tremendous freemasonry between national and regional museums, one which is not perhaps reflected in such a public forum as the Museums Association, but rather in the specialist working groups of the Association and in the Conference of National and Provincial Museum Directors (which meets annually). Neither the national nor the provincial museums could function without mutual help and trust.

1.5   Apart from minor gripes, I have found all regional museums which have received loan material to be grateful and deeply appreciative of the specialist help and co-operation provided by the nationals. Typical is an unsolicited comment made by the Hunterian Art Gallery in Glasgow concerning the British Museum's loan of the exhibition entitled *Avant-Garde British Printmaking 1914–1960*, which had previously been shown in London:

Not only was the quality of the show outstanding it was accompanied by well-designed and highly informative labelling which helped to introduce the general public to unfamiliar work and encapsulated the scholarship revealed at greater length in the catalogue to the complete show, a publication which will

be an outstanding reference source for the period for many years. Our deal-
ings with the Department of Prints and Drawings and the Design
Department were extremely satisfactory.

1.6   This report is a snapshot. It was perforce produced in less
than two months and could not, therefore, be based on deep and
long considered research; it is intended to provide an impression of
attitudes and possibilities at a time of political reorganisation of the
official arts structure with the creation of the Department of
National Heritage and the prospect of a national lottery. I have also
inevitably turned my attention towards the ironing out of misconceptions on the part of both the national and regional museums and
galleries. I hope that my own history in a major national museum
will not colour the result too strongly.

2 Towards a Definition

Categories of exhibition

2.1   It is possible to identify six main categories of exhibitions relevant to this report:

2.1.1   A major exhibition created specially for one centre wholly loaned by a national museum. Such an exhibition may sometimes be supplemented by material from the borrowing museum (as was the case with the loan by the British Museum – on two separate occasions – of *Lindow Man* to the Manchester Museum).

2.1.2   A major exhibition created specially for one centre with material drawn from a number of sources including national museums (as for example the exhibition *The Crossroads of Asia* at the Fitzwilliam Museum, Cambridge).

2.1.3   An exhibition of important material from a national museum loaned to two or three centres and either returned to base between showings or couriered by national museum personnel between the venues (as for example *Edo: Art of Japan 17th–19th Century* lent by the British Museum to two major centres).

2.1.4   An exhibition created for four or five centres and often provided with show-cases. It can be of top quality material, as witness the Royal Armouries' *Civil War* exhibition.

2.1.5   Small travelling exhibitions of low value material which can be circulated in sealed cases and handled by curators other than staff of the national museums. An example of such an exhibition might be *Living Arctic: Hunters of the Canadian North* toured by two area museum councils for the British Museum. A similar type of exhibition is that which is checked from time to time by the staff of the lending museum. *The Dinosaur Roadshow*, at present being toured by the Ulster Museum, is a case in point.

2.1.6   Screen exhibitions which demand little security and which can be displayed both in museum and in non-museum venues. Most of the Imperial War Museum loan exhibitions are of this character and travel widely.

All these categories refer equally to three-dimensional and two-

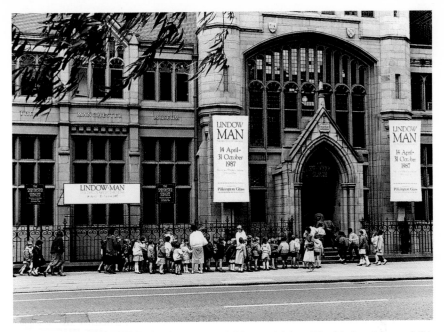

The popular face of loan exhibitions. Children visiting *The Lindow Man* exhibition at the Manchester Museum.

dimensional material. It is basically the first four that form the subject of this report.

2.2   I cannot emphasize too strongly that this report is only concerned with loans involving the national museums. Many exhibitions are mounted in the regions which have no input from the national museums (or at least only a minor element). These probably comprise the majority of exhibitions in regional museums; their organization, and the function of the Museums & Galleries Commission in relation to them, has not been considered here.

'Travelling' exhibitions

2.3   The brief for this report laid some emphasis on a consideration of 'travelling' exhibitions (basically the fourth category above). This term entered the general terminology of the Museums & Galleries Commission as a result of the report in 1983 of its working party on museum travelling exhibitions, a report based on a study undertaken to examine the situation after the suppression of the Victoria and Albert Museum's Circulation Department. In its literature concerning grants for exhibitions, the Commission defines travelling exhibitions as *exhibition[s] in two or more venues in the UK*. The rubric also includes the limitation that *One-off, temporary exhibitions are not eligible [for grants]*.

2.4   The Commission is in danger of painting itself into a corner by using this term in relation to its grant-giving activities. Although this condition has already been breached (for example the Commission grant-aided the National Gallery's loan in 1992 to a single centre, the Abbot Hall Art Gallery and Museum in Kendal), it remains a constraint on one of the Commission's main objectives in supporting exhibitions, namely the encouragement of access by the provinces to the collections of the national museums.   Many exhibitions can and should only be mounted in one venue, for reasons which can vary from considerations of conservation to those of cost.   Such exhibitions include some of the most exciting potential loans from the national museums.   The national museums are enthusiastic to extend the practice of making one-off loans.   It would, therefore, be sensible if the Commission were to drop this rubric and the idea that lies behind it (changing the title of its Travelling Exhibitions Unit to 'Loans Unit').

2.5   In this report, I propose to use the term 'loan' to cover all types of external exhibition activity, from the lending of individual items to a single centre to the type of circulating cased exhibitions of my fifth category above.

Loans of individual items

2.6   I was asked to look at the provision of loans of individual items to the regions.   I take this not to include the loan of a major single item as an exhibition in itself (of the type – such as the exhibition of a major new acquisition – delineated in my third category), but rather to relate to objects loaned to exhibitions arranged by regional museums. I have not included this type of loan as a separate heading in the categories listed above as it is a normal amenity of all museums (save those inhibited by statute or conditions of foundation from lending items – as for example the Wallace Collection).   Apart from frivolous or jokey requests, national museums will normally lend single objects to exhibitions in the regions if the venue can provide satisfactory security and conservation conditions. The National Gallery, for example, turned down none of its 217 requests for loans from within the United Kingdom in 1991–92, whilst turning down 57 of 154 requests from abroad.

2.7   The equivalent figures for the Victoria and Albert Museum show that 25 United Kingdom requests were refused out of a total of 808. By comparison, it is interesting to note that in the same period 47 objects were refused to foreign museums out of 177 requested. The aggregate of refusal of loans in the British Museum is not easy to recover because the documentation of such refusals (although seen by the Director) is filed departmentally. However, the figures for individual objects lent by the British Museum in the same period is 1276 loans to 35 centres in the United Kingdom and 714 loans to 49 centres abroad.

2.8   An important group of individual loans are the long-term loans made by the nationals to fill relevant gaps in the collections of regional museums. Local archaeological and topographical material is particularly significant here (the National Museum of Wales pays particular attention to this type of loan), as are portraits (the National Portrait Gallery is extremely generous in this respect). Long-term loans mean a lot to the regions and – so long as the material is inspected and the loans formally renewed at regular intervals – should be encouraged.

2.9   Other than the obvious limitations of conservation and security, there are two constraints on all loans. The first concerns the period of notice required. Most lending museums require at least six months' warning of a requested loan (more if it is a complicated multiple loan). This demand is not frivolous or bloody-minded. A loan often requires a considerable amount of work on the part of the lending institution. Permission may have to be sought from trustees (who may meet infrequently), security and conservation conditions have to be investigated and approved, conservation may have to be undertaken, photography arranged, packing-cases built, and staff made available for couriering and mounting duties; finally, it will be necessary to ensure that the item will not be on loan elsewhere at that particular time. Borrowing museums, therefore, should be willing to accept conditions of timing of this sort, particularly since they can usually obtain informal information as to the likely outcome of any loan request. As any exhibition takes well over six months to plan, and the list of proposed exhibits is one of the first things to be compiled, such a period of notice should cause few problems.

2.10   The second constraint is one of staff resources. The growing demand for individual loans from the national museums is putting increasing strain on staff resources, as all loans have to pass through different labour-intensive processes – from curatorial department to packer, by way of conservation and photography. In addition the curator in the lending institution is often asked to write the caption or catalogue entry and to travel with the object to the borrowing venue. Some measure of the size of the problem may be gauged from the fact that the Victoria and Albert Museum lent 808 items in 1991–92 for exhibition to 93 institutions in this country alone – a considerable logistical problem.

2.11 Discussion with directors of national museums has emphasized the increasing difficulty of finding resources to deal with this on-going and expanding burden. The Victoria and Albert Museum's estimate, which I have already quoted, of £250,000 p.a. as the real cost of servicing loan exhibitions is an indication of the total cost across the national museum and gallery community.

How exhibitions are constructed

2.12 Exhibitions can be initiated in a number of ways. First, a national museum can suggest that an exhibition already shown centrally could be lent to a regional centre or centres. This is more commonly done than is realised, for the arrangements are often made through the two bodies without outside referral. It is comparatively easy for the museum to remove such an exhibition from display in London or elsewhere and transport it in whole or part to the regions. This is also a comparatively cheap option, and one that most national museums would like to encourage. It is cheap because the research has been done; the catalogue has been published and the graphics and other two-dimensional and education-related material is easily transferable. Examples of such exhibitions are the Victoria and Albert Museum's watercolour exhibition entitled *Recording Britain* and many of the Imperial War Museum's photographic shows. In a few instances, an exhibition is shown in the provinces before being mounted in a national museum. The British Museum's *Chinese Bronzes*, shown at the Burrell Collection in Glasgow and at the Sainsbury Centre in the University of East Anglia is an example. Such exhibitions are of major importance. Often they show material not normally seen outside the capitals, and they should be enthusiastically encouraged – possibly above all other classes of exhibition.

2.13 More expensive is the provision of an exhibition which has been specifically created by a national museum for display in an individual regional museum. Such a show was the Royal Armouries'

16

Bradford's exhibition, *Warm and Rich and Fearless*, at Walsall Museum and Art Gallery. About half the loaned items in this exhibition came from the Victoria and Albert Museum.

loan to the Guernsey Museum of *Court Armour of Elizabeth*, all costs of which were met by the borrower. More frequent (but by no means numerous) are similar loans funded by the national museum. An example was the exhibition *Gandhara: the Art of the Monasteries* lent by the British Museum to the Sainsbury Centre of the University of East Anglia.

2.14   An important type of exhibition – and one which is to be encouraged – is that where the borrowing institution conceives, organizes and mounts a display on a specific subject with the help of a considerable national museum input. For example, Bradford and Walsall showed *Warm and Rich and Fearless* which contained 43 exhibits – about half the total – from the Victoria and Albert Museum.

2.15   Another manner in which an exhibition can be assembled is by a national museum recognising a perceived need for an exhibition and planning, curating, designing and mounting it themselves. The Royal Armouries' exhibition celebrating the 350th anniversary of the Civil War is a case in point.

A major loan. The Royal Armouries *Civil War* exhibition at Hull. Photograph by courtesy of the Board of Trustees of the Royal Armouries.

2.16   Finally, a number of national museums circulate to the regions, to as many as fifteen centres – in sealed show-cases or as photographs on screens – low-value, but nonetheless interesting exhibitions (because of their low security requirements these are sometimes made available to institutions other than museums – libraries or technical colleges for example).   Many of these exhibitions are toured by area museum councils or local museum services, which charge a small fee for the service.

3 Perceived problems

Circulating exhibitions

3.1 Taste and the demands of the museum-visiting public change imperceptibly. One year's raving success is next year's flop. Unfortunately the perception of what is needed and what is provided sometimes does not keep pace with the speed of change. Some still hanker after the type of circulating exhibition which flourished so splendidly in the years after the war. But is there room for such nostalgia? The closing of the Victoria and Albert Museum's Circulation Department in 1977 was at the time seen as disastrous; it caused fluttering in dovecotes throughout the country and shock-horror stories in the national press. The then chairman of the Museums & Galleries Commission saw it as *a setback to the development of friendly relations between the rich and splendid national museums and the hundreds of smaller museums in the provinces*. Yet the closing down in April 1992 of the much smaller but similar service provided by the Science Museum (howbeit since 1981 circulated at arm's length through the Tyne and Wear Museums Service) was accomplished in deafening silence – nobody apparently misses it, and the Science Museum is consequently able to save some £38,000 p.a.

3.2 The existence of dedicated loan collections of the type once provided by the Victoria and Albert Museum has now been totally abandoned, and a vast if somewhat *ad hoc* network of loan exhibitions to regional centres has grown up and works successfully. Some of these exhibitions are orchestrated by the area museum councils, but in some cases they are organised directly by the national museums.

3.3 Regional taste has become more sophisticated since the days of the Circulation Department. There is a clear demand for more sophisticated material and better graphics – for exhibitions which relate more clearly to the region or which highlight important elements of regional museums' collections. Larger regional museums mount successful and highly original exhibitions which have an academic and popular importance as great as any seen in London or Edinburgh (*The Vikings in England* at the Yorkshire Museum for example). The nationals willingly lend superlative pieces to such exhibitions and give generously of their time and expertise to support such projects. Thirty years ago national museums were inhibited from such support. Loans like that made to the major exhibition, *Romanesque Art c.1050–1200 from collections in Great Britain and Eire*, in Manchester in 1959 were rare; now they are commonplace. Museums, regional and national, have changed considerably. Where there was an assumption of refusal to requests for loans, there is now a presumption of agreement. Circulating exhibitions originated by the Victoria and Albert Museum and the Arts Council prepared the ground for greater expectations.

3.4   The Arts Council's touring exhibitions service still exists, although remodelled as part of the South Bank Centre. It is now the only national institution which features loans to provincial centres as a central plank in its service policy. The form and function of this loans service has changed drastically over the years, and has happily kept pace with changing demands. But the services provided by the South Bank Centre must be seen as entirely dissimilar to those provided by the national museums; for the Centre is not in any real sense a museum, it simply has some museum-like functions.

The function of a museum

3.5   It is important to understand the function of a museum. A museum exists primarily in order to collect and preserve material for posterity and to make that material available to the public at all levels from the scholarly to the "cor blimey". In making its collections available to the public through loans to regional museums, the national museums and galleries fulfil part of their duty of accessibility, for they have a public duty to their sister institutions in the regions. Their collections are held in trust for the whole nation and indeed have often been purchased by the nation – through a museum's purchase grant, by the National Heritage Memorial Fund, the National Arts Collections Fund or similar bodies – or symbolically given to the nation by individual donors. The collections do not belong to the fat cats of the south-east or to the centrally-funded museums at Cardiff, Edinburgh or Liverpool; they are the property of us all. To do them justice, the national museums and galleries agree to this proposition, even if they vary in the manner in which they express it.

3.6   It is difficult to generalize concerning the national museums and galleries. All have different problems, different priorities, different organisations and classes of collection. Their attitudes towards loans consequently vary, not so much because they do not believe in loans, rather because of the problems they face in delivering them and in the conception they have of the type of loan they feel able to provide. This is perhaps the reason for the widely-held canard that national museums in general are inconsistent, penny-pinching, bureaucratic and even bloody-minded in their attitude to loans to the regions. Such accusations are largely untrue and unfair, and it is important that they are seen to be so.

3.7   Certain differences between museums are patent to professionals, but only dimly perceived by the layman. They may indeed be ingredients of the misconceptions concerning the attitude of national museums to the regions. Two distinctions are crucial:

3.8   First, there are museums which – while they may be structured in departmental form – basically deal with a single class of object. Most typically, art galleries (for example the National Gallery) belong to this group, but some military-based and specialist museums (for example the Royal Armouries) can also be classed under this heading. Such museums usually have central records and a registrar to look after them and, to a greater or lesser extent, central expertise. This centrality can facilitate requests for loans.

3.9   Second, there are the multi-departmental museums (the National Museums of Scotland for example) which historically have departmental records and expertise that cannot be controlled at the centre. This means that loan processing must fall on departmental staff who have many other duties to perform, and this is an expensive process. This is particularly noticeable in the case of the Natural History Museum, where each department issues its own loan forms.

3.10   Museums (art galleries particularly) holding collections which consist of only one or two kinds of material (for example painting and sculpture) differ from those which deal with a broad range of materials – from, say, drinking glasses to motor cars. The packing, moving and mounting of material in the former group is fairly standardised, whilst these activities can cause horrendous problems in museums of the latter group. (One might here contrast the Tate Gallery and the Science Museum.)

3.11   These distinctions are fundamentally important in any attempt to expand the loan activities of the national museums, in that the cost of planned expansion is very different in the two groups of museums. Although in all cases any growth in loan services must inevitably depend on the provision of extra staff, it is generally cheaper to organise an exhibition of painting or other graphic art (which not only usually comes from an institution with a centralized registry, but also requires little more than a wall and a bag of nails to mount!) than one which demands the placing of three-dimensional objects in show-cases. There is, however, a considerable demand for this latter type of exhibition and both the national museums and the Museums & Galleries Commission wish to encourage them.

'Treasures in attics'

3.12 One specific canard must be dismissed. It is often stated by apparently intelligent individuals that the attics and cellars of national museums (indeed of all museums) are stuffed with treasures which lie dusty and forgotten, a monument to the avarice of successive generations of curators. As with all misconceptions, this one encompasses an element of truth. The attics and cellars of practically all museums and galleries contain material which is not normally put on public display.

3.13 The reasons for this are manifold, but material is generally held in store for one of two reasons. First, some material is too fragile (in all senses of that term) to be displayed. Thus watercolours are normally kept away from the light and displayed only for limited periods of time – and then only in strictly controlled lighting conditions.

3.14 Second, some of the material is basically archival, interesting mainly to the scholar. Thus bird-skins, held in considerable numbers in natural history museums or in departments of natural history, are (even by the aggregate of their numbers) of interest to researchers at a series of levels – be that researcher a taxonomist, geneticist or the local ornithologist. In the field of the applied arts or in history and archaeology, large typological series of drinking-glasses or flint axes are fundamental to scholarly research – the bigger the sample the better. In fine art, a fair number of engraved portraits, for example, are not perceived to be particularly pleasing aesthetically, but are of consuming fascination to scholars on a number of planes, being frequently used in exhibitions to illustrate everything from the perceived appearance of a person to the history and economy of printing or of interior design.

3.15 Much of this stored material would appear boring and repetitive to the non-specialist. Notwithstanding such perceptions, even some of the most dreary material can be used to advantage – as witness the very successful exhibition of works from the Chantrey Bequest loaned by the Tate Gallery to Sheffield. A museums' collections can best be compared to an archive. No single person is going to look at every object, but the fact that the objects are held safely and made available is of importance to a wide range of scholars, both amateur and professional, as well as to the generally curious.

3.16 Collections held in reserve are not neglected or forgotten. They are registered, curated and frequently consulted. Good museum practice (and the United Kingdom's standards in this respect are as high as any in the world) insists that objects in store should be looked after with the same care as material on display, with regard to security, conservation and documentation. Further, reserve collections are not closed to the interested public, but are open to study to anyone – amateur or professional – who wishes to have access to them.

3.17 It would be idle to deny that constraints of exhibition space are not (at least in part) responsible for some treasures being kept in store. But apart from those objects which would physically suffer if they were placed on display (textiles and watercolours are prime examples of this class of object), many of them are merely awaiting the refurbishment of a building or gallery. In the interim, there is often a real possibility of such parts of a collection being placed on loan. There is no reason, for example, why the Benin bronzes at the British Museum (which are scheduled to go on display in two or three years time) should not be loaned judiciously, as has been done with certain oriental series during the major refurbishment of the Museum's galleries. The Victoria and Albert Museum has indeed suggested that this might be one of the ways in which they could increase their loan service.

3.18 Although this is clearly a reasonable suggestion, it is not without problems, since the experts who would be needed to assemble and mount such an exhibition would already be working overtime to get the new permanent exhibition on display to a set timetable. It is, however, a promising area for expansion of loans to the regions; but it would cost money!

3.19 Some parts of national collections are seen in the regions at specially constructed out-stations. In some cases, these satellites are dictated by the size of the exhibits: the Science Museum has placed its railway collections at York (South Kensington has little space for this sort of rolling-stock); the Imperial War Museum holds its aircraft at Duxford (not to mention an enormous battle-cruiser in the Thames), whilst the Scottish collection of aircraft is held at East Fortune. In a few instances – the National Museum of Photography, Film and Television at Bradford is an example - a specific part of a national museum's collections, which would not otherwise have been displayed, has been established outside London to the great benefit of the public. A similar plan to move part of the Indian collections of the Victoria and Albert Museum to Bradford is under consideration. The Royal Armouries plan to move their main activities to Leeds, whilst retaining a toe-hold in the Tower of London.

3.20 This latter decision has met with some criticism, and indeed the establishment of an out-station is not a panacea – either to relieve space problems or to serve the regions. An out-station can be expensive of both staff time and money, and could sometimes be handled in a different way. It could be argued, for example, that the job presently being done by the Tate in Liverpool could be carried out more cost-effectively by the National Museums and Galleries on Merseyside (one of the constituent parts of which, the Walker Art Gallery, has a considerable and internationally-famous collection of modern and English painting and well-qualified staff to service it). In general, the foundation of an out-station (as indeed the foundation of any new museum) should be a matter of last resort. It is much better to make the national collections available to the regions by means of long-term loans to fill gaps in permanent exhibitions or through temporary loans of a circulating or one-off nature.

4 Costs

4.1   Loan exhibitions cost money – hard cash. They are also expensive of staff time. Some measure of the cost of organising a touring exhibition from a national museum can be estimated on the basis of the successful *Civil War* exhibition which is being lent to five centres by the Royal Armouries. The Armouries spent about £86,000 in cash on mounting an exhibition which was largely contained in six dismountable show-cases, but which also included an extensive graphics component. This sum did not include in-house staff time – either administrative or curatorial – nor conservation or design costs. It did include the cost of the exhibition catalogue, an education pack, transport and the cost of couriering the show.

4.2   The exhibition was seen by a large number of people in the provinces (55,000 in Hull, for example), and it is conceivable that those museums which charged for entry made a small surplus, but they had to bear the costs of such items as increased warding and security, publicity (other than the cost of producing the poster) and a certain amount of redecoration, electrical wiring and carpentry. They may have had to pay for extra teaching staff, local events (such as re-enactments of a Civil War battle) as well as local publicity, an opening reception and so forth. When the exhibition was shown at Hull, costs (over and above the £5000 hiring charge) amounted to £4681. At Coventry the cost to the local museum amounted to £9780 (it is difficult to compare the two sums, as certain costs in the case of Hull appear to have been carried by the Council; Hull appears not to have had to pay overtime, which amounted to some £3000 at Coventry).

4.3   This exhibition could not have happened without sponsorship (*The Times* contributed £55,000) and without a fairly hefty contribution from the borrowing museums supported by grants from the Museums & Galleries Commission. The Royal Armouries have estimated that the total cost of the exhibition to them (inclusive of staff time) was more than £120,000 (of which as we have seen they received some £86,000 as income). This figure is totally realistic of the resources which need to be committed for a sophisticated exhibition of moderate size.

4.4   Figures of this nature are not easy to obtain, but this order of cost can be checked to some extent against the published costs of another touring exhibition, *The Art of Lego*. Despite its misleading title (admitted by its organisers to be a mistake), this was a serious exhibition intended to demonstrate the influence of this constructional toy in the history of art and design. It was conceived and organised by the Clwyd Arts and Exhibitions Service (which, although not attached to a museum, has much experience of touring the visual arts). Before the exhibition opened at its first venue it had cost £120,000 and the touring process added another £60,000. Much of this cost was covered by sponsorship and hire fees at £3000 per month. The financial and cultural details of this exhibition are very different from those of the *Civil War* show, but they do demonstrate that such costs are realistic, and indicate that a six-figure sum must often be found before a major three-dimensional exhibition can be put on the road.

4.5   Such figures are very much in line, for example, with those quoted by the Yorkshire and Humberside Museums Council, who have kindly provided me with general figures concerning exhibition costs:

Our most recent exhibition, consisting of nine showcases, graphic panels and an introduction stand cost over £22,000 to produce (including staff costs). It used existing cases, therefore saving the £12,000 that would be required to build new ones. It will probably cost £15,000 to tour it for one year. A larger exhibition, using new cases, panels, audio visuals, etc., would cost at least £75,000 – £100,000. A really high quality one, employing inter-actives, computers etc, could easily cost £250,000.

4.6   Exhibitions of the 'blockbuster' type which are normally only found in capital cities are sometimes mounted in the regions.   An example was the exhibition *The Vikings in England*, which was shown at the Yorkshire Museum in York for six months in 1982, after previous showings at Copenhagen and Aarhus. This was a most expensive exhibition, the true costs of which have never been published. The total cost of mounting it in all three venues certainly exceeded £1 million at 1982 prices (although much of this must have been recovered by way of entry charges). This exhibition could only have been realised through the active and hands-on sponsorship of Times Newspapers Ltd together with financial input from a series of British and Danish firms, foundations and official bodies. That it was successful is demonstrated by the fact that it had 320,000 visitors at York. Such exhibitions – which clearly depend on considerable support from the national museums – are rarely mounted outside London, but they are not impossible to realise and should not be lost sight of (such exhibitions are still occasionally seen today – as witness Birmingham's exhibition of Dutch painting, *Images of a Golden Age*).

4.7 There is, however, no reason why medium-sized exhibitions of the size and cost of the Royal Armouries' *Civil War* show should not be mounted more frequently, provided that resources of both cash and manpower are available. Because of limitations of space, the Royal Armouries does not mount special exhibitions within its own premises at the Tower of London (although they hope to mount such exhibitions when they move their operations to Leeds) and, consequently, have little need to use their staff, cash or sponsorship for in-house exhibitions of a non-permanent nature.

4.8 This is very different from the situation of other national museums. The British Museum for example – which may mount some fifteen or twenty in-house exhibitions of varying sizes in the course of a year – has simply not got the staff resources to provide outside touring exhibitions on this scale, as it has to service its own permanent and temporary exhibition programme. Nor has it the cash to buy staff in. The British Museum – and others in like cases – understandably feels that it is difficult enough to obtain sponsorship for in-house exhibitions. It does not have the resources within its existing fund-raising activities to find money for loan exhibitions.

4.9 Similarly, major provincial museums – as for example Birmingham City Museum and Art Gallery which has a long tradition of providing splendid exhibitions and has just mounted a major Poussin show – work hard to achieve sponsorship for exhibitions which they themselves have the expertise or the will to show. Smaller provincial museums can also do this – a remarkable series of archaeological exhibitions has, for instance, been mounted by the Scunthorpe Museum – but too often in cases like this, local sponsorship is of too small a nature to be able to cover realistic exhibition costs. It is at this point that grants from the Museums & Galleries Commission become invaluable (the Scunthorpe Museum received a total of £7,500 in grants from the Commission for *The Barbarians* exhibition). The Commission, however, whose total grants for 1991–92 amounted to £109,000 (see Appendix B), can only realistically provide seed money for major exhibitions.

4.10 Not all exhibitions are – or need to be – as expensive to conceive and mount as that which celebrated the Civil War. Exhibitions of pictures (what museum professionals love to call 'flat art'!) do not demand the kind of elaboration needed to display three-dimensional objects. All that is normally needed in the borrowing institution is wall space and security; and space can be provided more often in smaller provincial museums than in the great municipal museums – and provided quite cheaply. The estimated cost of mounting the Tate Gallery's exhibition, *From Turner's Studio*, in eight centres in 1991–92 was only £28,000. It would be quite possible, for example, to mount a major exhibition of paintings at the Ilkley Museum for little expense beyond transport and extra warding, but it would cost a very considerable sum to mount a cased show in the same dedicated exhibition space.

4.11   Equally, the excellently-designed and extremely versatile show-cases used by the Sainsbury Centre at the University of East Anglia at Norwich cut the cost of mounting a three-dimensional exhibition considerably, and have been the reason why some very successful loan exhibitions from national museums have been shown there (see Appendix F). Few museums have such splendid equipment. The Sainsbury Centre's show-cases were provided by the benefactors, who took (and continue to take) a keen and detailed interest in its practical functioning. Publicly-funded regional museums have seldom been able to afford such specialised equipment. This is a pity as it is, for example, arguable whether Ilkley (which is in the middle of a major tourist area) might not attract more visitors for a loan exhibition than the Sainsbury Centre (which is in the middle of a university campus and not entirely easy of public access).

4.12   Major regional museums can occasionally mount important exhibitions with little expenditure by using their existing resources. Co-operation with the British Museum provided the Norfolk Museum Service at little cost with a remarkable exhibition of the Snettisham Iron Age treasures at the Castle Museum, Norwich, in 1991–92. In this case, staff costs on both sides were the most important element of expenditure, and both museums were willing to hide these. Other hidden costs were in-case security and graphics.

4.13   The declared costs of this particular exhibition are of interest. The British Museum paid out £1955 and the Norfolk Museum Service £2796. Of these sums the largest element was photography: Norwich paid £1530 for the photographic prints, whilst the British Museum picked up the cost of the negatives, £1816. In this instance, it was possible to show local treasures of national importance in the

Benin Man and Metal in Ancient Nigeria loaned from the British Museum to the
Sainsbury Centre, University of East Anglia. Investment in standardised, easily erected
show-cases has been a major element in attracting loan exhibitions to the Centre.

main museum of the region in which they were found. Another example from the British Museum was the exhibition of the Iron Age bog body from Lindow in Cheshire at the Manchester Museum on two occasions. (The design and travel costs of a small number of British Museum loan exhibitions of varying character are given at Appendix E).

4.14   When a great deal of public money has been spent on an acquisition – as for example for such a painting as Holbein's *A Lady with a Squirrel and a Starling*, recently acquired by the National Gallery, or the *Armada Service*, acquired by the British Museum – it would seem fair to the taxpayer if they were shown at a number of regional centres before being put on permanent display in the purchasing institution. A tour in this spirit is now being arranged by the consortium of museums which bought the Holkham drawings, whilst in Scotland the *Dumfries Freedom Box* presented to Henry Dundas in 1793, which was purchased by the National Museums of Scotland with the aid of the National Heritage Memorial Fund and the National Art Collections Fund, was displayed in the Dumfries Museum. Preliminary (if informal) enquiry would suggest that in general the nationals would welcome such an opportunity. Such outreach would not be expensive.

To visit the provinces? It is suggested that major new aquisitions acquired with public funds should be lent to provincial centres before being placed on display in the purchasing museum. An example might be Holbein's *A Lady with a Squirrel and a Starling* acquired in 1992 by the National Gallery. Reproduced by courtesy of the Trustees, The National Gallery, London.

5 Problems and solutions

5.1   If it is accepted that there is a considerable demand for loan exhibitions (and I have many representations to this effect), it is clear that such a demand cannot be met without a considerable infusion of cash; but, before attempting to quantify amounts, other problems must be aired and solutions offered in order to cut potential costs and remove perceived difficulties on the sides of both borrower and lender.

What can the regional museums afford?

5.2   Regional museums are strapped for cash, even some of the biggest municipal museums are finding it difficult to keep open – as witness the Bristol Museums. There is, however, a great demand for loan exhibitions in the regions, and there is good reason why these demands should be met. Some measure of the lower end of the market in terms of cost may be gauged from the charges made for the exhibitions brokered by the area museum councils. Normal prices here vary between £250 and £500 per month, and many museums seem able to afford such a sum (the average length of such an exhibition is just over six weeks).

5.3   Loans from national museums do not come cheaply. Apart from photographic and couriering costs, which are mentioned elsewhere in this report, regional museums are frequently bothered by insurance and overtime costs. The Hunterian Art Gallery of Glasgow University, for example, in borrowing the *Avant-Garde* show from the British Museum found it difficult to find £557 for their share of the insurance and £1,250 for extra staffing – and this in a place which basically shows only 'flat art', for which this modern gallery has purpose-built showcases. Costs would have been much higher – due to mounting, transport and couriering costs – if an exhibition of three-dimensional objects were to have been borrowed.

5.4   What then can regional museums afford if they are to receive loans from the nationals? The Manchester Museum's comments on costs are of interest:

We would like to be able to obtain from the national museums exhibitions which are object-orientated, not just models and photographs, at a price reasonable for our sort of institution. I suppose a realistic price is about £1000 for a two-month showing, plus the onward cost of transport.

5.5   A sum of £2500 seems to be the maximum amount many small museums would be able to afford from their own resources (and that with the aid of local sponsorship) in order to be able to mount a special exhibition which contains a loan element – whatever the category of that exhibition might be.   Even this sum can be difficult to raise, but local funding could be supplemented by means of a grant from the Museums & Galleries Commission, if it had the money.

5.6   Local sponsorship may seem a vital enabling element in much exhibition planning; but in practice the sums achieved through sponsorship are generally slight.   In some big cities, industries or commercial concerns are willing to give substantial sums to major exhibitions, but this is by no means a general pattern.   National experience would show that – with the exception of the Royal Academy – sponsorship for exhibitions which contain a large three-dimensional element is not easy to find.   This is particularly true if the exhibition concerns history or archaeology rather than fine art. This is no less true in the provinces, and reliance cannot be placed by museums or by government on such funding.   It must be emphasized that it is the duty of the borrowing institution to find sponsorship; the lender is almost inevitably too involved in his own fund-raising campaign to be able to help in more than a generally supportive fashion.   Although the regional museum curator and his committee will have the best contacts for local sponsorship, it might be possible for the Museums & Galleries Commission to act as a clearing house for information concerning possible sources of both local and national funding.   Some chain-stores, for example, allow local managers a certain amount of freedom for sponsorship and the Commission should research and list such potential sponsors, paying attention to their preferences.

Curator and courier

5.7   There is a strong feeling – amounting sometimes to resentment – in certain provincial museums and (more particularly) in area museum councils concerning the fact that national museums insist on their own staff handling loan items.   This can of course be a costly process since a curator – and sometimes a technician – usually have to be present when objects are mounted in the exhibition venue. The provincial museums and some of the area museum services, not without reason, claim that they have staff trained to handle material of the same quality and delicacy as that which is being lent. National museum directors, however, point out that, as accounting officers, they are responsible to Parliament for the security and condition of their collections. Under law they cannot abrogate this responsibility, even if they wanted to. They point out that it is normal in international loans for the lending institution to send curators to handle the loaned objects. Only thus, if an accident occurs, can responsibility be assigned appropriately. They see no reason why the same practice should not obtain with regard to loans within Britain.

5.8   This practice is based on experience. Every national museum can relate horror stories concerning the mishandling of objects without authorization in the course of loan exhibitions. These vary from the loss of objects, the taking of unlicensed photographs (with the consequent loss of revenue in copyright fees), the dropping of pictures, even to the moving of a safe with a borrowed object inside it! Any curator who has ever taken part in the mounting or dismounting of a loan exhibition has experience of potential disasters, which have only been averted by the immediate exercise of curatorial authority. This is largely understood and accepted by most regional museums. Indeed in the last few years regional museums have followed the practice of the nationals with regard to their own loans; their staff accompany loans to most venues (including national museums) and charge travel and subsistence. The couriering of loans and the exclusive handling of material by the staff of lending institutions has become good museum practice.

5.9   It is clear that couriering sometimes gets out of hand. An example quoted by the Birmingham Museums and Art Gallery is, I hope, not typical:

The British Museum has always responded very well to our requests for loan, but borrowing from them can be extremely costly and complicated. Whilst the need for couriers is clearly understood, the BM demands that a courier from each of its departments lending to an exhibiting should accompany the loan; during a recent exhibition at Birmingham, twenty-eight objects (many of them small) from the BM were couriered by no less than six people from three departments. The travelling and subsistence costs thus incurred (with subsistence graded according to status) were very high...

Indeed!... Further, it must have been extremely expensive of the British Museum's staff time. Clearly this was an aberration and

From Turner's Studio: Oil Paintings and Oil Sketches from the Turner Bequest. A loan from the Tate Gallery to the Glasgow Art Gallery and Museum.

should not have happened. Partly this episode must have been the product of the multi-departmental structure of the museum, but partly it is a product of the fact that the British Museum cannot afford extra staff to co-ordinate loan requests, for it is certainly not true that the Museum insists on a courier from each lending department. Indeed, I have been informed that the British Museum has recently agreed to one courier travelling with objects from two departments to the Down County Museum – a considerable reduction in expense. There is, however, clearly a lesson to be learned in this context.

5.10 The cost of courier and technical travel and subsistence remains, however, an important element in all exhibition budgeting. Borrowing is often severely restricted in the light of such costs, even when arranging 'blockbuster' exhibitions in London. Borrowers should not, therefore, complain about costs; they should budget for them. There is, however, no reason why they should not attempt to reduce costs by negotiation. National museums will often give permission for their objects to be handled and couriered by staff of other lending nationals (arguing that the accounting procedures of all national museums are the same and that standards are similar).

This is not always the case, however, as loan practice is not necessarily the same. Nationals will occasionally permit other experienced institutions to handle loan material – the South Bank Centre in 1988–89 toured the successful British Museum exhibition, *Lost Magic Kingdoms and Six Paper Moons*, to six regional centres, and the Centre and the Museum are at present negotiating for a number of touring shows of prints and drawings.

5.11 Such permission can be extended to curators in provincial museums. The Tate Gallery in 1991–92 toured an exhibition *From Turner's Studio* to eight British centres. Although packing and transport were supervised by Tate staff, the local gallery's staff in all but one venue were allowed to do the hanging. It is arguable that directors of national museums could be more liberal in respect of couriering and handling, based on their judgment of the professionalism and experience of the borrowing curators. But the more important or delicate the object, the more carefully it should be handled – if only from a public relations point-of-view. At the end of the day, the directors of the lending museums are responsible for this material, and their responsibilities must clearly be seen not to have been neglected.

5.12 Both borrowing and lending institutions would be well advised to discuss all matters of handling of loans at the planning stage of the exhibition process, so that costs can clearly be budgeted and even negotiated down. It is useless to leave such matters to the last minute and then complain – this leads to bad feeling which may inhibit future loans.

5.13 An exhibition cannot be mounted without financial cost; thus a borrowing institution which cannot raise the wind has no business to be in the exhibition game. In this respect the ability of the Museums & Galleries Commission to make grants to borrowing institutions is of crucial importance. The Commission (see Appendix B) makes grants for general exhibition purposes, which can include the costs of couriers and technical assistance from the lending museum. National museums should consider whether they are not too rigid in some of their couriering and curatorial demands. In turn borrowers should budget for these costs.

Bureaucracy

5.14   One of the commonest charges made against the national museums and their handling of loan requests is that they demand too much paper-work. Thirty years ago, when the modern trend towards loans gained momentum, a loan was often negotiated by a simple exchange of letters; but as loans multiplied it became essential to document the movement of objects more carefully. The rising tide of conservation demands has resulted in further controls which can only be realized by the use of more paper. It is now common practice in multi-departmental museums to document the movement of objects even between departments. It is clear that museum curators now take a much more serious view of their responsibility for objects. Over the years, loan forms have been refined, and lenders have inevitably asked for more detail and have imposed more regulation on borrowers.

5.15   This has not been done without reason. Indeed the standard of documentation has proved so successful that British loan forms have been copied or adapted by museums and other institutions abroad – including the Council of Europe. There are now, however, a multiplicity of loan forms as each museum or gallery designs its own. Most forms ask similar questions and lay down similar demands slightly differently. Accusations of bureaucracy are, therefore, understandable. I would consequently recommend that the national museums should attempt to standardise their loan forms. In the case of galleries (and those departments of the Victoria and Albert Museum, National Maritime Museum and Imperial War Museum which deal with paintings) a slightly different loan form could be devised which might serve all such institutions. This would at least provide a rational and familiar form for all. Individual museums with individual requirements could attach an appendix listing special regulations if anomalies exist, but I would hope that these could be obviated by discussion at drafting stage and any unavoidable extra regulations kept to minimum length. The best forum for the creation of such standardisation would be the National Museums' Directors Conference and the standing consortium of administrative officers of the national museums.

5.16   Many museums charge for photography in respect of loans. This is needed for record purposes – but may also be used for publication or publicity. Everybody resents photographic charges and, as everybody takes photographs nowadays, there is a tendency to believe that photographs can be taken much more cheaply. This may be so, but the results are not consistent and if the cost of time is included it will be seen that this is nonsense – particularly insofar as national museums are concerned. Photography is expensive, but few exhibition cost-centres cause so much trouble and ill-feeling. The real cost of photography in relation to an exhibition can be considerable – an example of such costs has already been quoted in relation to the Snettisham Treasure exhibition at Norwich. Such costs are not exceptional and have to be borne by one side or the other, but there seems to be a consistent lack of reality among borrowers concerning them. Complaints are heard from all over the country. Manchester Museum, for example, was very sore that record photography cost £1353 for the exhibition, *The Ancient Olympic Games*, borrowed from the British Museum to support the city's bid for the modern Olympics. These are, however, real costs and, having followed up this case, I am clear that they were properly incurred.

5.17   There is a widespread belief that some museums (and the British Museum particularly) wilfully charge for photography whether a photograph exists or not. Whilst it should be explained that lending museums will generally need to have a separate photographic print on its loan file and that existing photographs are not always suitable for record purposes, there cannot in every case be a need to order a new negative. National museums should look at their practices in this matter and, if there is some truth in this allegation, should mend their ways and charge only for that element of photography which is really necessary.

5.18   Conversely, it should be clearly understood by borrowing institutions that there are costs attached to loans and that photography is one of them. (In justification of the British Museum's case it should be said that the Museum has thoroughly researched the cost of photography, and its charges are based on the true cost of the service – photography is not subsidized.) It would, however, be fair to ask national museums to provide an estimate of the cost of photography at the time when they are approached for a loan so that this charge could be budgeted for. ·

5.19   A few museums (the Royal Armouries for example) charge a handling fee for loans. Whilst this may be justifiable in relation to loans abroad (although many museums do not charge on grounds of reciprocity), it is felt by most national museums to be a deterrent to borrowers, and charges are not generally instituted. As the collections are public property, supported by taxpayers' money, it would seem equitable not to charge; but borrowers should remember that

all questions asked of a lending institution – even details for catalogue entries and the like – cost curatorial time and consequently
money, and that such services may have to be paid for.

Insurance and indemnity

5.20   The government indemnity scheme has been extended to
regional museums acceptable to the Museums Security Adviser.
There are consistent complaints that 1% of the indemnity figure has
to be covered by the borrowing institution. I see no reason, however, why this charge should be removed. The fact that museums have
to find the cover should be a reminder that they are dealing with
valuable objects and have responsibility for their safety while they
are on loan. In most cases, this cover can be achieved relatively easily and at minimal cost to the borrower by an extension of existing
insurance policies.

5.21   It is a nonsense that a national museum does not get full compensation as of right, on the loss or damage of an object which it has
lent to the regions and which is covered by indemnity, whereas a private or non-national owner does. Further, if the national lends an
item which has been accepted in lieu of tax, the promise of compensation is only in respect of the amount of tax settled, which is normally much less than the open market value at the date of the loan.
This must be cleared up by the Treasury, as it is a clear disincentive
for the nationals to tour.

Conservation

5.22   Conservation is king! Loan forms contain many conditions
laid down by conservation officers. These vary from levels of relative
humidity and lighting to the kind of material used in the construction and embellishment of show-cases. Such regulations are a nui-
sance, but are mostly reasonable and are here to stay. Most lenders
insist on a conservation report on every object which is to be lent
and (while in many cases such reports are almost formal – in dealing
with stone axes for example) these reports sometimes recommend
that conservation be carried out before the object is fit to travel.

5.23   Some conservation requirements are expensive. The question
of who is to pay such costs must, however, be addressed. The
answer is not always easy. Some objects, for example, can safely be

left in their existing environment without conservation, but might need treatment before they may be safely moved out of a building – such objects are usually composite items made up of different materials, or are objects which have elements which could shake to pieces if moved over any distance. If the item is not deteriorating physically in its home museum, the cost of any treatment to enable it to travel should be borne by the borrower. The lender should, however, be expected to pay if the item is in a state of active deterioration. This should be common ground.

5.24 Other decisions are not so simple. Cosmetic ones particularly. It is not an especially good advertisement for a museum if it lends an object which, for example, seems dirty. Such dirt can be honourable – the grubby protective mount of a much-studied drawing for example. Many museum curators, however, will not wish to see their items displayed in such conditions and, if they were to put it into one of their own exhibitions, would naturally have the mount cleaned. A minor operation of this sort can cost staff time – albeit often minimal. Who then pays if a loan request is received? Equity would suggest that the cost should be carried by the borrower, but discussion may often persuade the lender that such cleaning should be done free of charge. Such minor treatment is often not even acknowledged, and the lending museum bears the cost without comment. But borrowers should recognise that in such circumstances they depend on the good-will of the lender. If a requested loan carries with it conservation costs, the borrower should put up or shut up – he should not cry foul.

5.25 There is a consistent, loud and seemingly justifiable complaint by curators in both national and regional museums that conservation standards vary from one museum to another – often quite considerably. This can be infuriating to the organiser of an exhibition. Conservation demands are now so well documented that it would not seem unreasonable to ask conservators to get their act together and provide consistent standards of conservation demands for exhibition organisers. There is a role here for The Conservation Unit of the Museums & Galleries Commission. The Commission should call a conference to plan for the standardization of conservation criteria for different classes of object. This is clearly no easy task, but it would be a sign of professional maturity if conservators could establish agreed standards. If such agreement could be reached it would, incidentally, have international implications which could only be beneficial.

Planning and budgeting

5.26   There is nowadays a great deal more realism about planning exhibitions. This particularly applies to matters of timetable. It has already been pointed out that most national museums ask for at least six months' warning of loans. They would also prefer to have pre-liminary notice of likely requests well in advance – the sooner the better. Otherwise there can be complications. The Prints and Drawings Department of the British Museum, for example, may make a loan within this country or abroad once a fortnight – it can, therefore, sometimes be difficult to provide loan services at the required time, and some adjustment may be necessary.

5.27   Once permission for a loan has been granted, a process is set in train in the lending institution which might involve the services of up to four or five members of staff handling the object over the peri-od leading up to the exhibition. Cancellation of a loan request (which happens all too frequently) is, therefore, a waste of resources, and does not leave the lending body in the happiest frame of mind. To this end, all details of venue and finance should be settled before application for loans are made. If it is clear at this stage that the costs of borrowing appear too expensive, then a decision to cancel or trim must be made.

5.28   Conservation and security aspects of any exhibition should if possible be worked out beforehand – perhaps with the aid of the Museums & Galleries Commission – so that permission to borrow can more easily be granted. Most national museums will insist on a report from the Museums Security Adviser before a loan request is granted, and (because physical conditions change with some fre-quency) they normally will not allow the fact that a building has received security clearance in the recent past to extend that clear-ance automatically. Clearance is referred back to the Museums Security Adviser. This is a cumbersome procedure and it might be worth the Museums Security Adviser consulting his colleagues in the national museums to see if any sort of rolling programme of security clearance would be acceptable to the directors as accounting officers. In considering such a move it might be borne in mind that the prac-tice of obtaining security clearance for every loan is breached in spir-it in relation to long-term loans, which are often renewed without referral to the Museums Security Adviser. It would be worth investi-gating the possibility of compiling a register of museums which have security acceptable to the Museums Security Adviser. Such museums could be issued with a certificate renewable, say, every two years.

5.29   At the end of the day, proper budgeting is the key to the smooth running of a loan exhibition. It is clear from practically all that has been said so far in this report that this is the area of loan exhibitions most fraught with difficulty. All museums are experienced in budgeting; proper costing should, therefore, cause few difficulties. From Day One of the planning process, it is essential to consider and plan for costs. Ill-feeling will be engendered with the lending institution if, because of inadequate budgeting, it is found that there are insufficient funds to meet all the costs of an exhibition and that modifications have to be made at the last minute. Similarly, it is not fair to complain after the event concerning costs charged to borrowing museums for justifiable and budgetable costs laid down by the lender in advance. The Travelling Exhibitions Officer of the Museums & Galleries Commission should be given the task of making himself familiar with the normal charges made by the national museums, so that he may advise the borrowing museums accordingly.

5.30   In some, but not all, museums the total planning and budgeting of a loan exhibition is left to a single curator. This is unfair. The curator of a loan exhibition should be helped and monitored by an internal committee which should impose checks and balances so that expenses do not run away with a project; further, the committee should support him so that he does not become bogged down in detail. The director of the borrowing museum should, as a matter of course, chair the committee and should be present at all meetings, together with the appropriate design, conservation and financial advisors. It is important that the director be involved in this process, as the high public profile of temporary exhibitions can be of great political importance in terms of the standing of the museum with its public; if there are problems the museum can suffer and in such a case the director will be blamed.

How long should an exhibition last?

5.31   I have received many representations to the effect that the current practice of mounting an exhibition in a regional centre for a period of six weeks or so is wasteful of resources – in that the period is too short. The Circulation Department of the Victoria and Albert Museum initiated this practice which has been continued by the South Bank Centre and the area museum councils. This is alleged to provide the maximum benefit from loans, and is said to ease the lender's burden in arranging transport. I am unconvinced by such arguments.

5.32   In the case of major exhibitions this period is clearly far too short, as indeed it may also be for many exhibitions arranged through the area museum councils. Publicity for an exhibition only takes off as a result of press interest which usually results from a report on the opening. Thus nearly a week may be lost before it enters local consciousness. More importantly the educational element of an exhibition generally cannot achieve its full potential against such a time-scale. Ideally an exhibition should always extend into school holidays so that families may visit exhibitions and so that teenagers in the run-up to national examinations (who rarely visit exhibitions in school groups) may have an opportunity to see them. General inertia means that many exhibitions go unvisited until the last minute. Six weeks is too short a period to overcome this endemic disease and many sufferers do not consequently see the exhibition.

5.33   From the point of view of a national institution which lends an exhibition of major importance, the hassle of mounting and dismounting a show for such a short period is hardly worthwhile. Exhibitions in the national museums – and indeed in many of the great municipal museums – normally last for between three and four months, and there seems no reason why the short period which is the norm in the regions should not be extended. There is likely also to be a commercial spin-off if this were to become normal practice.

Design

5.34   The most expensive element of any exhibition, other than staff costs (which are normally not quantified), usually lies in the design and construction of the show. In most cases where a loan exhibition from a national museum is envisaged, it will probably be most economic to use the national museum's design staff, as few regional museums have design offices. Depending on the amount of material to be shown, the time taken by designers to create an exhibition need not be very great. On average, seven weeks of designer time (both graphic and three-dimensional) would be needed to provide graphics and to design in-case mounts and lay-outs. To this would need to be added a preliminary site visit and possibly supervision of the mounting of the exhibition. But – as is the case with curatorial staff – space has to be found within a design office's programme to accomplish this. Consequently an exhibition has to be planned well in advance (two to three years). Naturally it is possible to use a freelance designer for this purpose, but this is certainly more expensive and puts extra demands on curatorial time in both borrowing and lending institutions. If extra money is to be found for loan exhibitions, some of it will have to be diverted to this area.

5.35 The design will naturally depend on the perceived construction of the exhibition. An elaborate purpose-built exhibition will demand more supervisory time of the designer, but an exhibition using existing cases (belonging either to the borrower or to the lender) will be much less expensive of design time. A few national museums have show-cases which can travel, and it might be worth researching the type of cases available commercially and also examining the viability of creating a central pool of information concerning the whereabouts of such furniture.

5.36 The life of show-cases which would meet the security demands of the lenders is likely to be rather short. It is desirable, therefore, (and certainly cheaper) to use show-cases held by the borrowing museum and to tailor the exhibition to what is available. Some major regional museums might find it worthwhile to build up a modular system of 'clip-on' exhibition equipment which can be adapted to a wide variety of exhibitions. (A model might be found in the system used over many years at the Museum of Mankind – which, although now collapsing of old age, has been in use for twenty years.)

5.37 Design plays an important part in the planning process of temporary exhibitions. Any museum which is planning to construct an exhibition with a major loan element from a national institution should ask for advice on design at an early stage of planning. A national museum should be able to provide this advice free or at minimal cost. Such advice would be a sensible use of national museum resources and should result in savings all round in the long term.

Retailing

5.38 No present-day exhibition can be mounted without a commercial spin-off, by the sale of catalogues, postcards, replicas and associated material. This is the least well researched area of loan exhibitions, and I have found it difficult to gain any general view of practice or profits. The planning of the commercial activities associated with an exhibition is rarely seen as a matter of urgency, and is frequently left until the last moment. The lead-time for the produc-

Purpose-built travelling show-cases designed by the British Museum.

tion of suitable souvenirs, however, can be long. Further, while a regional museum may be able to buy in from a national museum, the type of merchandise (and particularly its cost) which can be sold in the regions is different from that which can be readily sold in London with its large numbers of international tourists who appear ready to spend money on a grander scale. Whilst certain costs can be shared – postcards and catalogues for example – it is not clear where such shared retailing is most effective. In relation to catalogues, there is evidence that the more expensive publications of the type normally produced for London exhibitions (£12.95–£15.95) do not sell in the regions, whereas low-priced catalogues (£3.99–£4.99) do. As considerable sums of money may be involved in producing suitable souvenirs, research should be carried out into this and other commercial elements of loan exhibitions; I would, therefore, recommend that a specialist consultant be called in (possibly funded by the Museums & Galleries Commission) to examine this much neglected subject.

Information

5.39   Information about the availability of exhibitions toured by the area museum councils is available through the newly initiated publication, *Touring Exhibitions from Area Museum Councils 1992–1995*. I trust this publication will continue. It lists fifty-nine exhibitions, but includes only two or three offered by national museums (one at least of which is not acknowledged), and one – *Underwater Archaeology* – has been arranged by collaboration between the National Maritime Museum and the Area Museum Council for the South-West.

5.40   The Museums & Galleries Commission has set up an on-line database, known as MagNet, which supplements the information in this booklet with information on exhibitions organised by other institutions. MagNet has not as yet been made fully operational but is being used experimentally by a pilot group of twenty-five institutions. Subscribers are able not only to retrieve information, but can input details about their own exhibitions directly into the database; they can also revise entries at will. Further, they have access to up-to-the-minute information concerning the availability of exhibitions not yet on any published list and can search the database for subject, size, cost of hiring and degree of protection required (a typical entry is printed at Appendix C). The database does not provide information about national museums' loan exhibitions, although it intends to do so.

5.41 This is a laudable project but seems an over-elaborate method of providing information and in some ways duplicates the information provided by the area museum councils. It is also comparatively expensive to subscribers. A modem suitable for automatic dialling costs £200 and ongoing costs may vary between £90 and £100 per annum. I cannot see that there will be enough continuing demand in any one institution for such information at this price, particularly as most museums would want to consult it at most once or twice a year, and would probably not be sufficiently disciplined to keep it up-to-date. It is no part of this report to question this system, but it is clearly reasonable to extend the database to provide information about all exhibitions – current and projected – mounted by museums and galleries in the country. The system could be so programmed that it could provide hard copy for circulation to museums and other interested parties. It would give excellent publicity to all loan exhibitions. It might be possible to amalgamate it, both as a catalogue and a record, with the area museum councils' list.

The role of the area museum councils

5.42 The area museum councils are keen to get involved in touring exhibitions from national museums. They have indeed a well-developed infrastructure for touring – particularly of medium- and small-sized exhibitions. They have in the past toured (and occasionally still tour) sealed-case or screen exhibitions of low commercial value for the national museums (sometimes handling and mounting the material as agents of the nationals). They do this well, but charge the local museums a fee for doing so.

5.43 There is some criticism of the area museum councils' charges from regional venues, which should be addressed. It is, however, almost certainly less expensive for the nationals to have small exhibitions toured by the area museum councils (despite the fact that they may not want to charge the regional centres), and this system should – if funding allows – be developed. Further, there is no reason to believe that the area museum councils are not competent to handle such loans – as is sometimes apparently alleged.

5.44 It would seem, however, that there is no argument to suggest that area museum councils should play a major role in mounting larger and more specialised exhibitions from the national museums of the kind which have been highlighted in this report. They are certainly competent to handle such shows, and some museums may wish to make use of their expertise (some area museum councils are, as I have pointed out, eager to undertake such work). But most nationals have a great deal of in-house expertise; so that curatorial, conservation and administrative considerations all point to greater efficiency without a middleman.

The role of the Museums & Galleries Commission

5.45   In 1991 Richard Wilding reviewed the policy and financial structure of the Museums & Galleries Commission for the Minister for the Arts. One of his recommendations (10.11) was that:

Unless greatly increased resources can be put into it, the Travelling Exhibitions Unit should be wound up after appropriate guidelines have been produced, and the resulting saving applied to other MGC purposes.

To this the Commission replied:

We have made a bid for greatly increased resources, and attach importance to the Unit continuing to operate on the present modest scale until these resources are secured.

Wilding pointed out that the potential demand for a *fully-grown exhibition system* was higher than existed at the time of his report. He further reported widespread complaints concerning the efficiency of the unit – its grant-giving policy was obscure, no clear guide-lines were given to applicants, good applications were capriciously rejected – but concluded that the reasons for this were that the Unit was under-resourced.

5.46   Although no extra resources have been forthcoming, the Unit is still in existence, and still – after reviewing its policy – continues to give grants. The Unit costs about £150,000 p.a. to run. More than half this sum – £109,000 – was spent in grants in 1990–91, the balance comprising salaries, overheads, etc. In the last financial year, then, a further 20% was spent on exhibitions than during the period Wilding had under review. It is clear from these figures, and from the dedication that the Commission continues to show to the idea of loan exhibitions, that the Commission does not wish to phase out the Unit, although the start-up grant provided by the Office of Arts and Libraries ran out in 1991 and grant applications were temporarily suspended during 1992–93 following publication of the Wilding Report.

5.47   The Unit has a staff of two and is formally controlled by a committee chaired by a Commissioner. Much of the work of the Unit is initiated by the officer in charge of it, who has worked very closely with many of his clients and has managed to build up good relations with one or two of the nationals – no easy task! He is responsible for all Commission liaison concerning loan exhibitions, and has inaugurated the MagNet database described above which, although up and running, has yet to be proved as a viable system.

5.48   It is clear that on the basis of such slender resources the Unit is overstretched and cannot itself organise exhibitions. Whilst it was able to provide seed money for the *Civil War* exhibition circulated by the Royal Armouries, it has little experience of working directly with national museums. Although there seems no reason why the Unit should not continue with such useful experiments, it needs more resources to deal with them.

5.49   The Commission recognizes that the national museums are the key to an expanding exhibition programme – particularly in relation to three-dimensional exhibits and high-profile, high-value shows. It should therefore, through Commissioners, encourage the nationals in whatever way possible to increase and expand their loan activities in the regions. It could also, by publicising the national museums' activities as regards loans to the regions, help the nationals to dispel criticism of their attitudes. Further, the Unit could encourage regional museums to take loans from the nationals and push the idea that the best loans are those which only travel to one or two centres.

5.50   Certain suggestions have been made in the course of this report concerning proper functions which could be undertaken by the Travelling Exhibitions Unit of the Museums & Galleries Commission. All of them point to the Unit chiefly as a disseminator or coordinator of information, as for example in an increased use of its MagNet database, in the suggested advice on sponsorship, or in setting up a national conference on conservation standards. The Commission should become a centre of information about exhibitions: about their availability, financing, budgeting and the general mechanics of setting up an exhibition. It would also serve a useful function by producing an annual publication of forthcoming exhibitions in both the regional and national sector.

5.51   In its 1991 report, *Local Authorities and Museums*, the Museums & Galleries Commission stated (in the section entitled 'Funding Considerations' paragraph 6.23) that:

*The normal range of grants, between £1,000 and £10,000, is too small to
make a significant contribution to touring by the national museums which, as
far as [the Office of Arts and Libraries] was concerned, was the main reason
for its funding. Equally the budget is too small to halt the decline in touring
by the area museum councils, and this was not, in any case part of its original
purpose. The scheme has been most successful in assisting the middle range of
museums, especially in the form of cost-sharing collaborations between museums of similar size and resources.*

It is clear that there was a difference of perception between what the
Commission felt should be done with limited funding and what the
Office of Arts and Libraries hoped might be achieved. The only way
forward seems to be to persuade the Department of National
Heritage (the successor to the Office of Arts and Libraries) to provide the national museums with sufficient funding to enable them to
provide loans from their collections, which they could easily do without third-party mediation.

5.52   Ultimately the Commission should withdraw from aiding
regional museums for this purpose, but it would be fatal to stop
making grants towards this objective before sufficient money is made
available by the government to the national museums. Even modest
grants enable some regional museums to obtain loans from the
nationals. A withdrawal of grants would defeat the chief object of
the original exercise so far as the Office of Arts and Libraries was
concerned. Funding to the regions for loans by national museums
should, therefore, continue *ad interim* at the present level.

5.53   I believe that the Wilding Report was mistaken in suggesting
that the Unit should be closed down. It was, however, right to say
the Unit could not continue to function in its present form. The
most cogent reason for retaining the Unit is to provide the seed
money for loan exhibitions of all kinds in the regional museums. A
measure of the help given by the Commission's grants is clearly
shown in Appendix B: some of the most exciting regional exhibition
projects would have been stymied without this financial help and
moral support. The Unit has a future.

5.54   I feel that the committee which regulates the Unit should be
broader based by being strengthened by the inclusion of a senior
officer (at curatorial grade 5 level) from one of the major lending
national museums, a member of staff of similar level from a university museum and the director of one of the large municipal museums.

50

5.55 I would add a footnote to this section; it has been represented to me that quite a number of museums in Scotland do not meet the Museums Security Adviser's criteria for loans from national museums. I am sure that the same is true in some cases in other parts of the country. For very little investment this could be rectified, and the Commission is ideally placed to provide the relevant advice.

The position of the national museums

5.56 The gap left by the closing of the Victoria and Albert Museum's Circulation Department was never properly filled. As a direct result of the closure of this department, the British Museum, within a very limited budget, started to lend a series of exhibitions of both three-dimensional and two-dimensional material of first-rate importance (Appendix D). There never was any case for recreating the Circulation Department, and it now cannot be reinstated as its collections have been dispersed – in some instances to other museums. Rather the British Museum initiative of lending prime pieces has been welcomed by other national museums, who have copied and adapted it according to their own circumstances. Some of these exhibitions have been extremely elaborate, as for example the exhibition, *Vasna, Past and Present*, which recreated a section of a Gujarat village in the Leicester Museum, but which was too expensive and too fragile to send to other centres.

5.57 For the moment this seems to be the best way to bring material from the national museums to the regions. The Victoria and Albert Museum has put a toe in this water, for example by touring the exhibition *Recording Britain* which had been previously shown at South Kensington. The National Gallery and the Tate have also initiated loan exhibitions of important material (although the Tate has recently had to suspend this service due to lack of cash).

5.58 It should be emphasized, as has been indicated elsewhere, that a major exhibition can be mounted at less cost if it has already been shown, as the research, catalogue, graphics and conservation are already available (thus the National Museums of Scotland are showing *Rae of the Arctic* in Kirkwall in 1993). Similarly, loans of material taken off display during the refurbishment of a gallery can also be lent economically of staff time, as the material will already have been well researched and new label copy prepared. Exhibitions specially constructed for showing in the regions are much more expensive.

5.59   As to smaller exhibitions, the Imperial War Museum and other nationals have frequently toured screen exhibitions, largely made up of photographic and information panels.   The British Museum and the National Maritime Museum have also toured exhibitions of low value material – usually in sealed cases – through the area museum councils.

5.60   An interesting extension of this type of exhibition are the *Discovery Rooms* of the National Museums of Scotland, which have been widely circulated to regional museums in Scotland following a start-up grant of £3,000 from the Museums & Galleries Commission. These interactive displays consist largely of handling collections which are attractive to children and adults alike.   One of this series, on Japan, has been bought by the Japan Festival for travel throughout the United Kingdom, and will shortly have its first showing at the Horniman Museum.   In this case the money received from the sale will be used to fund another travelling discovery room.

5.61   The establishment of out-stations has brought some of the national collections to the regions.   Particularly successful are the out-stations of the Imperial War Museum and the Science Museum and – to a lesser degree – of the National Museum of Wales and the National Museums of Scotland.   The Tate Gallery Liverpool has been a success, although I have argued above that this would probably be better served if its administration was transferred to the Walker Art Gallery (part of the National Museums and Galleries of Merseyside).   But out-stations are expensive to run and generally the national museums – and the country – would be better served by lending to existing institutions.

5.62   Unfortunately, all national museums are under strong financial pressure and have to strain their resources to feed outreach of the sort the regions need.   The regions have even less money. Signs of this shortage of cash are evident in the cut-backs which are starting to take place.   The Science Museum's priorities at the moment cannot allow it to replace its touring exhibitions; the Tate Gallery has suspended its touring exhibitions; the British Museum has severely reduced its budget for lending exhibitions to the regions.   Further, (although it has little to do with the national museums) it is symptomatic that the number of touring exhibitions offered by the area museum councils is shrinking.   The only national museums which are expanding their loan practices are the National Gallery (where the exhibitions can be quite cheap to administer, as they largely consist of paintings and graphics which are not expensive to mount given the right security and environmental conditions) and the National Museums of Scotland, which are doing so as they start to get over the traumas caused by amalgamation.

5.63   The will to increase access by lending to the regional museums is enthusiastically present in all national museums. The National Army Museum, for example, would like to initiate a series of exhibitions concerning military campaigns of the Second World War, exhibitions which could travel to museums in parts of the country where regimental ties with such campaigns are particularly strong. The National Maritime Museum is actively planning to tour part of its successful *Pirates* exhibition. There is some interest in the possibility of touring recently acquired major treasures and it might be possible to ask for subsidy to do so from the National Heritage Memorial Fund or the National Arts Collection Fund who could thus publicize their work. These and many other projects are being considered by the national museums and all of them would be welcomed in the regions.

5.64   But the shortage of money is real. The resources of the national museums are stretched almost to breaking point. They do their best to fulfil what they see as their obligation to lend to the regions, but the administrative, conservation and curatorial time involved grows as more demands are made upon the lenders. Servicing loans takes time away from museum duties which are central to caring for the collections – the fact that museums are reducing their lending activities illustrates this perception. In some cases, staff resources have been stretched to the limit – and almost beyond it.

5.65   In speaking to directors and senior officials of most national museums, I have been left in no doubt that unless there is a considerable increase in resources to cover the cost of staff time they will have to cut their loans. The sum of money needed is not huge, but it is significant. Although there is some degree of variation in estimates of the amount of money needed to service growth in this area – for which there is clearly a demand – it would seem that the single department museums and galleries would need between £35,000 and £50,000 extra per annum and the multi-departmental museums between £100,000 and £150,000 extra per annum to service loans efficiently. The British Museum has kindly provided estimates of how such new money would be spent (Appendix E). In total a sum of about £1 million would be needed by the national museums to preserve and expand the loan service to the regions. If such money were forthcoming, it would need to be committed for some time –

and possibly ring-fenced – as the lead time in preparing an exhibition is measured in years.

The role of the regional museums

5.66   Regional museums vary greatly in size and the facilities available to them. Consequently the smaller museums tend to borrow the type of exhibition brokered by the area museum councils, while the larger museums – particularly the major municipal museums – are much more able to research and mount their own exhibitions and generally tend to do so. Major loan exhibitions originated in the national museums can be shown in either type of museum – and indeed this happens. This practice should be encouraged. The only problems concern standards of security and environmental control (which can usually be adjusted and are indeed much more standardized than they were) and the cost of extra staff and exhibition furniture.

5.67   Regional museums normally have excellent relations with the nationals and are consequently able to bid for exhibitions and loan material directly. There is no need for a marriage broker. The problems are mainly financial, and I have shown that even some of the larger museums find it difficult to find sums in the region of £2000 or £3000 in order to cover all the loan costs (this of course includes such elements as publicity and information as well as such normal costs as installation and travel). This money should be made available to them through the Museums & Galleries Commission until the national museum grants are increased – as they must be – as part of the loan service. The Commission should provide the regional museums with advice as to the availability of loans and the sort of conditions that may be laid upon them.

5.68   I would once again emphasize the importance of proper and realistic budgeting by the regional museums. In the past, lack of financial control has been the cause of many of the minor irritations felt by both lender and borrower.

6 Where do we go from here?

6.1 I have made a large number of detailed recommendations concerning the development of loans between national and regional museums. They are summarized at Appendix A. Some of them will save a little bit of money now, some might have some effect in the future.

6.2 But it is money that is the real problem. Real money! Despite the enthusiasm of the national museums to lend major items to the regional museums, their resources are shrinking and the demands made on them grow every day. They already provide the regional museums with many thousands of objects each year and, they have other objects in great numbers on long-term loan. They simply cannot afford to increase this activity, for which there is great demand. Indeed most national museums are cutting back on loans to the regions. Nor can the regional museums afford to pay the national museums for exhibitions – they are even less well off than the nationals.

6.3 The Museums & Galleries Commission manages nobly to keep alive a small series of grants which have helped to spread parts of national museums' collections around the country. But it has been very thinly spread, and most of its Travelling Exhibition Unit's resources have helped non-national museum exhibitions.

6.4 The standard of special exhibitions which continue to be mounted in the regions is higher than it has ever been – a standard second to none in Europe. The public is growing more sophisticated in its taste and – given extra resources – many more exhibitions of distinguished quality could be mounted.

6.5 The quantity and type of money needed cannot be met from private sponsorship, as most of it is needed to fund staff costs in the nationals. This has no glamour for potential sponsors. Nor can significant money be earned at the door. The only possible way to achieve a breakthrough in this area is through the provision of extra public money.

6.6 The Secretary of State for the National Heritage will shortly be introducing legislation to set up a national lottery to benefit sports and the arts. While it is clear that every possible arts body is putting in bids against this sum, there can be few objects more worthy of support than the encouragement of regional exhibitions of material held centrally for the nation in the national museums and galleries. This is one of the best ways of increasing access to the national collections.

6.7 The sum of money involved would not be great. It would be divided roughly between the national museums, in sums of the type indicated in paragraph 5.65 and in Appendix E. The national museums would also be responsible for funding some at least of the costs which would inevitably have to be borne by the regional museums. This then is the bottom line: the sum necessary to expand significantly the loan services of the national museums is £1 million.

Appendix A   Summary of recommendations

Central government should:

1. provide extra money to enable the national museums to consolidate and gradually increase their loan exhibition services: a global sum of £1 million is a realistic figure (paragraphs 5.65, 6.6, 6.7); and

2. remove anomalies in the availability of indemnities: a national museum should receive full compensation for any loss or damage; if an item accepted in lieu of tax is lost or damaged, compensation should be at the open market value at the date of the loan (paragraph 5.21).

The national museums should:

3. be enabled to provide loans from their collections and other assistance for major exhibitions in regional museums (paragraph 5.51);

4. show major acquisitions in the regions as a matter of course (paragraph 4.14);

5. lend major exhibitions already prepared for their own purposes or temporarily removed from display (paragraph 2.12);

6. make available more long-term loans (paragraph 2.8);

7. control couriering more strictly and reduce it to the minimum by means of inter-departmental and inter-museum co-operation (paragraph 5.10);

8. consider whether they can be more liberal in their demands on handling of loans by outsiders (paragraph 5.11);

9. standardize their loan forms (paragraph 5.15);

10. standardize conservation requirements for loans (paragraph 5.25);

11. examine their practices with regard to charges – particularly photography – made in connection with loans (paragraph 5.17);

12. provide, at the earliest possible opportunity and as a matter of course, an estimate of all charges likely to be incurred by borrowing museums (paragraph 5.18);

13. use their own design offices to design their loan exhibitions (paragraph 5.34);

14. cooperate in providing show-cases for loan exhibitions (paragraph 5.35).

Non-national museums should:

15. be encouraged to research and compile exhibitions containing a large proportion of loan material from national museums (paragraph 2.14);

16. consult their national colleagues at the earliest possible date in planning exhibitions (paragraph 5.12);

17. apply for loans at least six months ahead of the opening date of an exhibition (paragraph 2.9);

18. budget properly for loans (paragraph 5.29);

19. set up a committee chaired by the director to advise on each exhibition project (paragraph 5.30);

20. consider investing in modular movable exhibition furniture if they frequently mount exhibitions (paragraph 5.36);

21. plan showings for longer than six to eight weeks (paragraph 5.33);

The Museums & Galleries Commission should:

22. retain its Travelling Exhibitions Unit (paragraph 5.53);

23. grant-aid exhibitions whether they be touring exhibitions or exhibitions in a single centre, and change the title of its Travelling Exhibitions Unit to 'Loans Unit' (paragraph 2.4);

24. offer grants to cover the costs of couriering loans, until more money is made available to the nationals for their loan services (paragraph 5.13);

25. continue to provide the seed money for loan exhibitions of all kinds in regional museums (paragraph 5.53);

26. strengthen the present Travelling Exhibitions Committee to include more senior representatives of national, regional and university museums (paragraph 5.54);

27. serve as a centre for the dissemination of information concerning loan exhibitions (paragraph 5.50);

28. extend the MagNet database to include all loan exhibitions mounted in the United Kingdom, and amalgamate it with the list published by the area museum councils (paragraph 5.41);

29. set up a database to advise regional museums about sponsorship (paragraph 5.6);

30. streamline security validation of conditions in regional museums (paragraph 5.28);

31. consider what action can be taken to improve security in those museums which do not meet the criteria for accepting loan material from the national museums (paragraph 5.55);

32. appoint a specialist consultant to examine retailing opportunities associated with loan exhibitions (paragraph 5.38).

The area museum councils should:

33. continue to administer small travelling exhibitions from the national museums (paragraph 5.43);

34. not administer major loans from the national museums (paragraph 5.44).

Appendix B Travelling exhibitions Grants and payments by the Museums & Galleries Commission, 1988-92

	grant (£)	fin. year
Grants to organisers for whole tours		
Area Museum Council for the South West: *Great Sea Dragons*	1,700	89–90
Area Museum Council for the South West: *Megaliths*	1,500	88–89
Area Museum Service for South East England: *Joint exhibition project*	4,000 2,000	91–92 91–92
Banbury Museum: *Dynamic Folk Toys*	1,500	92–93
Bath, Museum of Costume: *Gloves for Favours, Gifts & Coronations*	5,000	89–90
Belfast, Ulster Museum: *Dinosaur Roadshow*	4,500	89–90
Bersham, Industrial Heritage Centre: *Gold I Gave for Iron*	4,940	89–90
Bradford, Cartwright Hall: *Ramayana*	10,000	89–90
Bradford, Cartwright Hall: *Warm and Rich and Fearless*	5,000 4,000 1,000	90–91 91–92 92–93
Bradford, Industrial Museum: *Brass Roots*	18,000	89–90
Bradford, Industrial Museum: *Jowett Jupiter*	10,000	89–90
Brighton, Museum & Art Gallery: *Angelica Kauffman*	20,000	89–90
Bristol, City Museum & Art Gallery: *Here Be Dragons*	4,000 4,000	90–91 92–93
Bristol, City Museum & Art Gallery: *Art of Ruins*	5,000 2,000 2,000	89–90 90–91 92–93
Council of Museums in Wales: *Furniture of Childhood*	11,000 1,000	90–91 92–93
Cardiff, Howard Gardens Gallery: *Abram Games*	3,500	89–90
Cheltenham, Art Gallery: *Good Workmanship with Happy Thought*	4,000 3,500	91–92 92–93
Coventry, Herbert Art Gallery: *Bulgarian Icons*	8,000	92–93
East Midlands Museums Service: *Showcase project*	10,000	88–89
Exeter, Royal Albert Memorial Museum: *Lifting the Veil*	2,500	89–90
Gateshead, Shipley Art Gallery: *Davidson's Glass*	5,000	92–93

	grant (£)	fin. year
Glasgow, Glasgow Museums on Tour	6,000	92–93
Hove, Museum & Art Gallery: *Eric Gill and the Guild of St Joseph & Dominic*	1,500	90–91
	1,500	91–92
London, Livesey Museum: *Great Rubbish Show*	10,000	90–91
	8,000	91–92
	4,000	92–93
Manchester, City Art Gallery: *New Look*	6,000	90–91
	11,000	91–92
	5,000	92–93
Manchester, City Art Gallery: *Midwinter Modern*	4,000	92–93
Newcastle, Laing Art Gallery: *Biba*	7,000	91–92
	4,400	92–93
North West Museums Service: *Gillow Chairs*	2,500	91–92
Norwich, Castle Museum: *One for the Pot*	4,000	90–91
	4,000	91–92
	8,000	92–93
Nottingham, Castle Museum: *Body Adornment*	5,000	90–91
	5,000	91–92
Prescot, Museum: *Enamelling*	1,800	91–92
	600	92–93
Preston, Harris Museum & Art Gallery: *100-Nil*	5,000	88–89
Royal Armouries: *English Civil War*	1,000	90–91
Scarborough, Crescent Art Gallery: *Fired Earth*	5,000	90–91
	4,000	91–92
Scunthorpe, Museum: *Barbarians*	5,000	91–92
	2,500	92–93
Shropshire Museums Service: *Mammoths*	15,000	88–89
South Shields, Museum: *Mr Greathead's Lifeboats*	2,000	90–91
	2,000	91–92
	2,000	92–93
York, City Art Gallery: *The Nicholsons*	5,000	88–89

Grants to venues for individual showings

	grant (£)	fin. year
Bolton, Museum & Art Gallery: *Everyday Life in Ancient Egypt*	1,000	91–92
Brighton, Museum & Art Gallery: *Country House Lighting*	4,000	91–92
	1,000	92–93

	grant (£)	fin. year
Cambridge, Fitzwilliam Museum: *Old Master Drawings from Chatsworth*	2,000	88–89
Cirencester, Corinium Museum: *English Civil War*	6,000	91–92
	1,500	92–93
Coventry, Whitefriars: *English Civil War*	2,000	91–92
	1,000	92–93
Edinburgh, Royal Scottish Museum: *Discovery Room*	3,000	88–89
Exeter, Maritime Museum: *Cruel Sea*	1,000	90–91
	500	91–92
Hull, Town Docks Museum: *English Civil War*	2,500	91–92
	1,000	92–93
Keighley, Cliffe Castle: *Living Wood*	2,500	90–91
	7,500	92–93
Kendal, Abbot Hall: *Classical & Picturesque Landscape*	2,500	91–92
Leeds, City Museum: *Bulgaria: Tradition & Beauty*	1,000	90–91
	1,000	91–92
Leeds, Temple Newsam: *Country House Lighting*	5,250	90–91
	3,700	91–92
	1,000	92–93
North of England Museums Service: *GAME pilot project*	8,300	91–92
Nottingham Castle Museum: *English Civil War*	2,000	91–92
	2,000	92–93
Worcester, Commandery: *English Civil War*	4,000	92–93

Feasibility studies, research and publications

	grant (£)	fin. year
Area Museum Service for South East England: *Pre-evaluation*	500	89–90
Brighton, Booth Museum: *Agate Masterpieces*	660	90–91
Civil War leaflets	1,135	91–92
Margot Coatts: *Blue Peter Mystery Objects*	2,040	89–90
Coventry, Herbert Art Gallery: *Bulgarian Icons*	1,000	90–91
Ironbridge Gorge Museum: *John Cooke Bourne*	2,000	91–92
Tom Learmonth: *Recycling*	1,100	88–89
London, Royal Armouries: *Exhibition sponsorship*	1,000	90–91
London, Royal Armouries: *Civil War Period coordinator*	5,000	90–91
	2,201	91–92
	1,000	92–93

	grant (£)	fin. year
MagNet (electronic bulletin)	2,436	88–89
	2,700	89–90
	6,928	90–91
	4,715	91–92
Manchester Museum: *Duke of Bridgewater*	500	88–89
Manchester University: *Time-Lapse Video*	2,122	89–90
Museum Development Unit: *1940*	2,334	88–89
North of England Museums Service: *Exhibition Space Survey*	5,000	89–90
Nottingham, Castle Museum: *Body Adornment*	5,245	89–90
Oldham, Local Interest Museum: *Parrots*	500	90–91
	500	91–92
Scottish Museums Council: *Leisure Learning*	3,000	88–89
Scottish Museums Council: *Touring Appraisal*	5,000	92–93
Touring Exhibitions Group: *Packing & Handling Works of Art*	685	88–89
Touring Exhibitions Group: *Needs Survey on Exhibitions of Science and Technology*	2,000	88–89
Touring Exhibitions Group: *Sharing the Costs of Touring Exhibitions*	1,200	89–90
Touring Exhibitions Group: *Using Touring Exhibitions*	1,200	89–90
Victoria & Albert Museum: *Display case airtightness*	2,500	89–90
West Midlands Area Museum Service: *Joint Catalogue*	4,000	91–92
Philip Wright: *Hiring Fees research*	2,500	88–89
Yorkshire & Humberside Museums Council: *Expanding the Impact of Touring Exhibitions*	4,500	89–90

Appendix C   Specimen entry MagNet database of Museums & Galleries Commission

Title: Inspirations
                Historic and Contemporary Embroidery

Description: Selections from the Embroiderers' Guild collection and contemporary embroideries

Notes:
Inspirations is a travelling exhibition displaying embroideries from the Embroiderers Guild Collection, and the contemporary embroideries they inspired; plus intermediate experimental stages. The exhibition aims to stimulate an interest in embroidery and encourage participation in the craft, whilst presenting embroideries as multi-faceted objects which can be the starting point for a variety of subject studies. As well as wall space the exhibition requires 2/3 display cases.

Tour Dates: From 01/04/93 to 31/07/93   (available)
                From 01/02/94 to 31/12/94   (available)

Size band   30 linear metres
Protection   Moderate Security
Cost band   £400 + VAT + 2 way transport

Organiser   Lynne Szygenda
Organisation   The Embroiderers' Guild
Address   Hampton Court Palace
                Surrey
                KT8 9AU
Phone   081–943 1229

Appendix D Exhibitions circulated in the United Kingdom by the British Museum

Exhibition	Year	Venues
1978–91		
Sculptures of the Parthenon (replicas and photographs)	78–81	11
Gandhara: The Art of the Monasteries	79–80	1
Princely Paintings from Mughal India	81–83	2
From Manet to Toulouse Lautrec (prints)	81–82	4
Edo: Art of Japan - 17th to 18th century	81–84	2
The Ancient Olympic Games (model and photographs)	81–91	9
Thunderbird and Lightning: Indian Life in NE North America		
South East Area Museums Service tour	82–83	8
Council of Museums in Wales tour	84–86	8
Yorkshire and Humberside Museums and Galleries Service tour	86–87	7
West Midlands Area Museum Service tour	87–88	5
Goya's Prints	83–84	5
American Prints	83	3
Schools Loan of African Material (multiple loans to schools)	84–87	1
Vasna: Inside an Indian Village	84–85	1
Trading Shapes: Islamic and Chinese Ceramics	84	1
Himalayan Rainbow: A Nepalese Textile Tradition	85	1
Sporting Life: An Anthology of British Sporting Prints	85–86	4
The Print in Germany 1880-1993	85–86	4
James Gillray the Caricaturist 1756-1815	85–88	4
The Precious Image: Buddhist Sculptures	86	1
Contemporary British Medals	86–87	4
Masterpieces of Ukiyoe	87	1
Ronald Searle: Medals and Drawings for Medals	87	1
Landscape through Time: The Human Impact on Britain 8000 BC to AD 1800	87	1

Exhibition	Year	Venues
Celtic Britain: Life and Death in the Iron Age *(500 BC to AD 50)*	88–91	10
Chinese Bronzes: Art and Ritual	88	2
The Rumbustious World of Thomas Rowlandson - The *Prints: 1774 -1822*	89–91	4
Living Arctic: Hunters of the Canadian North		
Area Museum Council for the South West tour	90–91	4
Area Museums Service for SE England tour	91–92	4
Living Buddhism: a Photographic Portrait	90–91	2
Samuel Palmer: Visionary Printmaker	90–92	4
Man and Metal in ancient Nigeria	91	1
Avant-Garde British Printmaking	91–92	4
Shadow of the Forest: Prints of the Barbizon School	93–94	4
Total number of exhibitions = 30	*Total venues 119*	

Not circulated by Loan Exhibitions Unit
(direct negotiations by curatorial department with venue)

1978–91

Lost Magic Kingdoms and Six Paper Moons (tour arranged by South Bank Centre)	88-89	6
Ceramic Art of the Italian Renaissance	89	2
Britain and the French Revolution	90	1
Lindow Man	Twice to Manchester	
The Snettisham Treasure	91	1

Appendix E   Design and travel costs of selected small exhibitions circulated by the British Museum

The British Museum has been the only museum which has consistently circulated three-dimensional exhibitions since the closure of the Victoria and Albert Museum's Circulation Department (see Appendix D). Appended is a small sample of the design costs of such exhibitions. This excludes curatorial, conservation and publication costs (and of course the costs incurred by the lending museums) but is published in order to give a rough idea of the order of cost of such exhibitions. Please note that the costs might have to be adjusted for inflation. I am deeply grateful to the British Museum for allowing the publications of these figures which are simply raw costs of one part of the loan exhibition process.

Chinese Bronzes

Loan to:
    (a) Glasgow, Kelvingrove: 17 Dec 87-Feb 88
    (b) Sainsbury Centre, Norwich: 20 Sept-18 Dec 88   (£)

3D items
—

2D items
Typesetting, photos production of information panels and labels for:
(a) 1st installation	1,563
(b) Additional costs for venue	663

Publicity
Production, printing posters
(a) initial run	1,162
(b) run on	137

Travel and subsistence
(a) 5 members of staff to Glasgow	436
(b) 6 members of staff to Norwich	583

Transport
(a) Objects to Glasgow (Wingate & Johnston)	1,225
(b) Transport to Norwich by BM van	—

Misc costs
Dyelines/photos	26

Total costs (a + b) = £5,795

Celtic Britain

Production of travelling exhibition transported by BM to venues

Loan to: Hull, Durham, Peterborough, Bristol and Doncaster 1987–91   (£)

3D items
Cost of panel system, lighting, protective coverings   5,874

A/V items
Hologram   863

2D items
Information panel production typesetting, photos, labels etc   5,759

Misc costs
Dyelines, photos   67

Publicity
Cost of initial posters (over-printing by venues)   1,420

Travel and transport
BM Personnel, hire vans, labour etc   985

Total costs   £14,968

Man and Metal in Ancient Nigeria

Loan to: Sainsbury Centre (graphics only) 1991   (£)

2D items
Cost of information, panels, labels   2,551

Publicity
Posters and leaflets   2,864

Travel and transport
by Dept of Ethnography   1,258

Total costs   £6,673

Artistic Circles: The Medal in Britain

Loan to: Fitzwilliam Museum 30 June–30 Oct 92   (£)

3D items
Fabric, materials   230

2D items
Typesetting & production of information panels and labels   2,290

Publicity
Production and printing of posters   1,619

Travel and subsistence
4 staff for 7 days   164*

Misc costs
Dyeline prints etc   70

Total costs   £4,373

* Note: excludes costs of use of BM van

Living Arctic

Production of travelling exhibition re-using cases and screens originally designed for Thunderbird and Lightning loan exhibition

Toured by Area Museums Services for:
  S W England (4 venues) 1990-91
  S E England (7 venues) 1992-93   (£)

3D items
  Materials for refurbishing cases and panels: paint, fabric   1,271

2D items
  Typesetting, photos, production of information panels and labels   4,329

A/V
  Cost of video tapes   713

Publicity
  Production and printing of posters   1,380

                                              Total costs £7,693

No transport costs to BM

Appendix F   Projected budget for the expansion of loan exhibition services by the British Museum

I am grateful to the British Museum for kindly providing me with rough budgets which would enable it to expand its loans of exhibitions to regional museums.

Our target would be to circulate about eight exhibitions a year of a mixture of types – large and small, three dimensional and two dimensional. About four new exhibitions being created each year. Some would be derived from British Museum exhibitions, others would be created especially for touring. We would estimate that this would mean that we would reach some twenty to twenty-five venues a year.

Given input from existing curators, public relations and education staff we would need three extra staff: two full-time – a touring exhibition administrator and technician – and two-thirds of the cost of a three-dimensional designer.

We would need about 400-500 square metres of space for production and storage [space which might be found when the British Library quits the Bloomsbury site – DMW], plus a security van for transport.

Annual costs to include the three staff, office costs, brochure, subsistence and transport, production of four new exhibitions of different types, posters and publicity would be approximately £125,000 in the first year, reducing to about £115,000 in subsequent years.

There would be an initial set-up cost in making ready and furnishing the preparation and storage area.

It should be emphasized that, even with the proposed administrator, there would be additional hidden costs in both the curatorial, educational and conservation departments. It might be necessary to fund temporary staff to relieve pressure in these areas during the preparation period.

It is clear from this statement that the British Museum would need a capital start-up grant and an annual additional grant of some £130,000. In the first year this sum might be the equivalent of the start-up grant.

Acknowledgements

I would like to thank in the warmest possible terms all those who have helped in the compilation of this report. I am particularly grateful to the directors of all the national museums and galleries who have given up valuable time to write or talk to me. I must also thank Mike Sixsmith of the Museums & Galleries Commission who provided me with a great deal of information and generally acted as a post-box with patience and forbearance.

The following individuals and institutions provided me with a great deal of information and comment and to them I am most grateful: from the national museums Margaret Hall, Jean Rankine, Geoffrey House, Jenny Chattington, Ian Stead, Sheila Brock, Suzanne Bardgett, John Edmundson, Gwyn Miles, Giles Clark, Gillian Lewis and Henrietta Usherwood; from regional museums Elizabeth Smallwood of the Birmingham Museums and Art Gallery, Andrew Millward of the Manchester Museum, Martin Hopkinson of the Hunterian Art Gallery, Anne Bone of the Chichester District Museum, Julia Holberry of the Stevenage Museum, Lesley Simpson of the Down County Museum, Jane Glaister of Calderdale Museums and Arts Division, Helen Lanigan Wood of the the Fermanagh County Museum and Bernadette Gillow of the Greenwich Borough Museum, Ian Brown of the Scottish Museums Federation, and Denise Morris of Oriel Ynys Môn; from other interested bodies, Mark Suggitt of the Yorkshire and Humberside Museums Council, W. M. Elliott of the Area Museums Service for South Eastern England, Richard de Peyer of the Area Museum Council for the South West, Aidan Walsh of the Northern Ireland Museums Advisory Committee and Isabel Hitchman of the Welsh Arts Council.

I am also grateful to the following for permission to reproduce photographs: the Trustees of the British Museum (page 45); the Trustees of the Tate Gallery (35); the Manchester Museum (13); the Trustees of The National Gallery, London (31); the Board of Trustees of the Royal Armouries (18); The Sainsbury Centre for Visual Arts, University of East Anglia and Michael Brandon-Jones (29); and Walsall Museum and Art Gallery (17).

Printed in the United Kingdom for HMSO
Dd 295280 11/92 C12 531/3 12521